W9-AOV-801

ideals®

EASTER

50 Years of Celebrating Life's Most Treasured Moments

Vol. 51, No. 2

Publisher, Patricia A. Pingry
Associate Editor, Lisa C. Thompson
Art Director, Patrick McRae
Contributing Editors, Lansing Christman, Deana Deck, Russ Flint, Pamela Kennedy, Heidi King, Nancy Skarmeas
Editorial Assistant, Laura Matter

ISBN 0-8249-1115-6

IDEALS—Vol. 51, No. 2 March MCMXCIV IDEALS (ISSN 0019-137X) is published eight times a year: February, March, May, June, August, September, November, December by IDEALS PUBLICATIONS INCORPORATED, 565 Marriott Drive Suite 800, Nashville, TN 37214. Second-class postage paid at Nashville, Tennessee, and additional mailing offices. Copyright © MCMXCIV by IDEALS PUBLICATIONS INCORPORATED. POSTMASTER: Send address changes to Ideals, PO Box 148000, Nashville, TN 37214-8000. All rights reserved. Title IDEALS registered U.S. Patent Office.

SINGLE ISSUE—$4.95
ONE-YEAR SUBSCRIPTION—eight consecutive issues as published—$19.95
TWO-YEAR SUBSCRIPTION—sixteen consecutive issues as published—$35.95
Outside U.S.A., add $6.00 per subscription year for postage and handling.

The cover and entire contents of IDEALS are fully protected by copyright and must not be reproduced in any manner whatsoever. Printed and bound in U.S.A.

ACKNOWLEDGMENTS

OUT-OF-DOORS from *RHYMES OF CHILDHOOD* by Edgar Guest, copyright ©1924 by The Reilly & Lee Co. Used by permission of the author's estate. SPRING IN NEW HAMPSHIRE from *SELECTED POEMS OF CLAUDE MCKAY*, published by Harcourt Brace. Reprinted by permission of the author's estate. Our sincere thanks to the following authors whom we were unable to contact: George Cooper for WHAT ROBIN TOLD; Laurence B. Jackson for SPRING; Mary E. Linton for FRONTIERS OF FAITH; Don Marshall for LOVE IN BLOOM; and May Smith White for EACH YEAR.

Four-color separations by Precision Color Graphics Ltd., New Berlin, Wisconsin.

Printing by The Banta Company, Menasha, Wisconsin. Printed on Weyerhaeuser Husky.

The paper used in this publication meets the minimum requirements of American National Standard for Information Sciences—Permanence of Paper for Printed Library Materials, ANSI Z39.48-1984.

Unsolicited manuscripts will not be returned without a self-addressed stamped envelope.

Cover Photo
ZEBRA SWALLOWTAIL ON DOGWOOD
Gay Bumgarner

Inside Front Cover
George Hinke

Inside Back Cover
Donald Mills

Little Crocus

Margaret Rorke

Little Crocus, poking through,
Would I were as brave as you!
You're the scout the tulips send
To report the winter's end.
Hyacinth and Daffodil
Fear the earth above is chill.
Underground the bulblets cheer
When they hear you volunteer,
You, who seem to have no fear.

Breaking ground with grass-like leaves,
You the snowy earth receives,
Smiling at your fragile form,
Smiling till itself is warm,
Warm enough to open up
Your tiny funnel-fashioned cup.
"All is well," you notify
Those for whom you are the spy.
Then they too push toward the sky.

Little Crocus, I can see
Size of courage isn't wee
Just because a plant is small.
You're the bravest of them all.
They in all the hues God made
Soon will venture on parade,
But I wonder what they'd do
Without you to lead them through.
Would I were as brave as you!

Spring

The tiny buds peek forth upon
   The tall and lofty boughs
And signal with their color
   That spring is coming now.

The tulips and the daffodils
   Spring from their winter bed
And fill us full of happiness
   As our hungry souls are fed.

The golden sun warms up the earth,
   The birds fly high with song,
And we realize since spring came last
   Was really not that long.

So we'll enjoy each sunny day
   From now till autumn's through
And wait for spring through winter's snow
   The world's life to renew.

Alfred Neil Ward
Croton-on-Hudson, New York

Be Still and Know That I Am God

"Be still and know that I am God,"
   You said one balmy night.
"Take time to watch the moonlit sky
   And see the clouds in flight."
And so I stopped and listened
   To the peepers as they sang;
I felt the dewy evening,
   As its silence round me rang.
The silence of your presence,
   The stillness of your peace,
Engulfed my very being,
   And my worries all did cease.

"Be still and know that I am God,"
   You said one stormy night.
"Take time to watch my fury
   And my lightning in its flight."
And so I stopped and listened
   As the strong winds howled low;
I saw the dashing raindrops
   As they fell to earth below.
And in the fierceness of the thunder,
   Your voice did loudly claim,
"Be still and know that I am God,"
   In the sunshine and the rain.

Sue Evans
North Berwick, Maine

Love in Bloom

Don Marshall

I didn't write, dear, yesterday
But planted flowers instead,
Some four o'clocks to mark our tryst
Beside the tulip bed;

And, just in case, forget-me-nots
Along the garden walk,
Where almost every Sabbath Day
We used to stroll and talk.

I didn't write, my dear, and yet
We'll count no wasted hours,
For after ink is faded, dim,
Our love will bloom in flowers.

Overleaf Photograph
NORFOLK BOTANICAL GARDEN
Norfolk, Virginia
Kevin Shields/New England Stock Photo

NURSERY IN EDGARTOWN
Martha's Vineyard, Massachusetts
Dick Dietrich Photography

Easter Sights and Sounds

Loise Pinkerton Fritz

The garden's filled with color—
   White, purple, yellow, red.
The Easter sun has risen;
   It'll soon be overhead.
The air is touched with springtide;
   The birds are on the wing;
From belfries o'er the country
   We hear the church bells ring.

Everywhere new life abounds;
   It echoes far and near.
It's evidenced in sight and sound;
   It fills the heart with cheer.
Like drinking rays of sunshine,
   Is Easter's meaning, true:
Christ has risen from the dead
   To bring us life anew.

Planting Beans and Memories

Kathleen Wynveen

Today the sun is shining;
　　Let's call our grandson Jay.
The beans are needing planting,
　　And it's a gorgeous day.
Of course the work goes faster
　　If we can plant alone,
'Cause we don't count the speckled seeds
　　And pick up every stone.

But we're not planting beans, you see,
　　To sprout up to the sky;
We're planting little memories
　　To grow as years go by.

So even though it takes more time,
　　We'll call him anyway.
We'll count the beans and pretty rocks;
　　We'll call it "planting day."

And sometime far along life's road,
　　We will recall the scenes:
Those sunny days we planted
　　Both memories and beans.

A SLICE OF LIFE

——Edgar A. Guest——

Out-of-Doors

The kids are out-of-doors once more;
    The heavy leggings that they wore,
The winter caps that covered ears
    Are put away, and no more tears
Are shed because they cannot go
    Until they're bundled up just so.
No more she wonders when they're gone
    If they have put their rubbers on;
No longer are they hourly told
    To guard themselves against a cold;
Bareheaded now they romp and run
    Warmed only by the kindly sun.

She's put their heavy clothes away
    And turned the children out to play,
And all the morning long they race
    Like madcaps round about the place.
The robins on the fences sing
    A gayer song of welcoming
And seem as though they had a share
    In all the fun they're having there.
The wrens and sparrows twitter, too,
    A louder and a noisier crew,
As though it pleased them all to see
    The youngsters out-of-doors and free.

Outdoors they scamper to their play
    With merry din the livelong day,
And hungrily they jostle in,
    The favor of the maid to win;
Then, armed with cookies or with cake,
    Their way into the yard they make,
And every feathered playmate comes
    To gather up his share of crumbs.
The finest garden that I know
    Is one where little children grow,
Where cheeks turn brown and eyes are bright,
    And all is laughter and delight.

Oh, you may brag of gardens fine,
    But let the children race in mine;
And let the roses, white and red,
    Make gay the ground whereon they tread.
And who for bloom perfection seeks,
    Should mark the color on their cheeks;
No music that the robin spouts
    Is equal to their merry shouts;
There is no foliage to compare
    With youngsters' sun-kissed, tousled hair:
Spring's greatest joy beyond a doubt
    Is when it brings the children out.

Edgar A. Guest began his illustrious career in 1895 at the age of fourteen when his work first appeared in the Detroit Free Press. *His column was syndicated in over 300 newspapers, and he became known as "The Poet of the People."*

Saucy Sunbeam

Donna Ann Radford

A saucy little sunbeam
Slid through my windowpane;
He sat down on my pillow
And meant there to remain.

"'Tis time for you to wake up,"
He whispered in my ear,
And as he tickled my face,
He filled the room with cheer.

So I hopped out of my bed
And slid my blue jeans on;
I had to dress so quickly,
Or else he would be gone.

We rushed out to the garden
And danced about with glee.
The dew was on the roses;
The sun beamed down on me!

Opposite Page
ROSE ARBOR
Original painting by George Hinke

Handmade Heirloom

Leaded-Glass Windows

Heidi King

Who has not marveled at the majestic brilliance of a cathedral's stained-glass window? Stained-glass windows date back to the twelfth century, but their rich beauty still inspires the artisans of today who craft beautiful leaded-glass windows. Using both clear and colored glass, with flat or beveled edges, artisans solder the carefully-cut pieces into dramatic and colorful patterns.

Although its origin is uncertain, the art of making leaded-glass windows may have evolved from the procedure used to make primitive enameled jewelry whereby bits of ground glass were joined with small pieces of metal. Through the past 800 years, the art of making stained glass has evolved slowly but persistently. Centuries ago, artisans had to color the glass themselves by adding metal oxides to molten glass. They experimented with everything from stale wine to raw potatoes to achieve different effects. Today's artisan, however, only has to venture to the nearest craft shop or glass store, select the colored glass desired, and solder the pieces together to create his or her own leaded-glass treasure.

The art of making stained glass was almost lost in the seventeenth century when King Louis XIII of France destroyed every glassworks in Lorraine, which was a region known for glass production. Thankfully, in the eighteenth century it became fashionable among wealthy families to salvage glass panels from former eras and install them into their homes. This was the first use of stained glass in places other than cathedrals and churches.

Perhaps one of the first uses of the beautiful stained-glass images was to educate church attendees in the Bible and church law. Even today, artisans often use symbolic images in their work. While some of the finest examples of stained glass are found in churches and cathedrals, the technique of making stained-glass treasures has become so much easier that many crafters now create beautiful pieces for their own homes.

Making a leaded-glass window is very similar to completing a puzzle. Working from a detailed pattern, the artisan cuts the glass with a glass cutter or a sharpened disk called a stylus. This is the most delicate step in making the image, but it can be mastered with patience. The artisan then carefully arranges the different colors of glass, following the pattern, and solders the pieces together.

Lead is the most popular medium used for solder, which is purchased in strips called *cames*. Another option is adhesive copper foil, which is an ideal solder for joining small, irregular pieces of glass. The copper foil was developed by Louis Comfort Tiffany, the stained-glass artist famous for his Tiffany lamps.

Using materials readily available at most arts and craft stores, anyone can create personalized keepsakes of stained glass. Some crafters create stunning leaded-glass windows for their homes using colors and patterns that have special meaning for them. Others craft pieces of glass as window hangings to give to family and friends. Regardless of size or shape, handmade pieces of leaded stained glass are prized not only for their beauty and artistry, but also for their personal sentiment. Leaded-glass windows are heirlooms to cherish from generation to generation.

Heidi King, a free-lance writer and designer, lives in Tallahassee, Florida.

Opposite Page
SPRING WINDOW
Jessie Walker Associates

COLLECTOR'S CORNER

Lisa C. Thompson

Rocks, Minerals, and Gemstones

Centuries ago, people began collecting stones for their imagined magical powers. A diamond, for example, was thought to bring love and today remains a symbol of love. Emeralds were thought to preserve domestic bliss, and turquoise to ensure prosperity. A ruby would protect from nightmares, and a bloodstone would heal wounds. While most people have abandoned the old superstitions, rock collecting remains a popular hobby today.

The varied terrain of North America is rich with rocks, minerals, and gemstones. If you're lucky, an exciting find may be lying in wait right in your own backyard. Several remarkable pieces, including diamonds, have been found all across the continent. A strange pebble found in West Virginia in 1928 turned out to be the largest diamond ever discovered in the eastern United

States—34.46 carats. It was unearthed by a horseshoe pitch gone awry. A well digger in Wisconsin uncovered a diamond only half that size, but still a remarkable gem. In Brooklyn, New York, a young boy's quartz specimen, when broken open, revealed ten pieces of gold.

These stories prove that you don't need a large bank account or extensive travel plans to acquire an admirable collection of rocks and minerals. With a prospector's hammer and a sturdy pair of boots, you can set out to explore an attractive site right in your state. Many state tourist bureaus and geological surveys publish materials which provide descriptions and locations of state minerals. Where permission is granted, quarries often yield interesting finds, as do coastal areas and even stream beds. Some areas of the United States are particularly well-known for certain minerals. At the Crater of Diamonds State Park in Arkansas, for example, you can search for your own diamonds and take home all that you find.

A mineral is a natural, inorganic solid with a definite chemical composition whereas a rock is really a cluster of different minerals; rocks, essentially, comprise the stuff of which the earth is made. Rocks and minerals can be tricky to identify, as anyone who has fallen for "fool's gold" will tell you. Minerals can be identified with the help of clues such as weight, hardness, color, luster, streak, cleavage, or fracture. A mineral is said to have cleavage when it breaks with a smooth surface in a definite direction. When a mineral breaks like shattered glass it is said to fracture. Some minerals, such as calcite, fluorite, and even diamonds, are fluorescent in ultraviolet light. Rocks can be identified by their mineral content as well as color, texture, structure, and acidity. Many rocks will fizz if touched with any acid, even household vinegar.

A mineral becomes a gemstone simply when humans place more value on it. Gems are a select group of precious minerals often called the flowers of the mineral kingdom. They are valued for their unique beauty and rarity. One defining quality of most gems is their hardness. Ideally, a gem should be as hard or harder than quartz to be sturdy enough for jewelry. Some gems that are softer than quartz are cherished nonetheless; opal, turquoise, and moonstone are examples. Another quality desired in a gem is durability. It should not cleave or chip in everyday use.

Rarity can have a tremendous impact on the value of a gem. The amethyst was at one time a stone highly sought after until a lode of enormous proportions was discovered in South America. When it was suddenly available in abundance, the amethyst's value quickly plummeted.

Quartz crystals are popular gemstones with collectors because of their variety and abundance. Quartz can be divided into two categories: crystalline quartz such as amethyst or rock crystal and general chalcedony such as agate or jasper. Yellow quartz, also called citrine, is especially popular and often sold as "yellow topaz" due to its similarity to the rarer gem.

Some gems are not minerals but rather products of living organisms; pearls, coral, and amber are examples, all of which come from the sea. A pearl forms when an oyster secretes the pearlescent material to coat an irritating particle inside the shell. Coral develops as marine skeletons collect calcium carbonate from the water to form islands or reefs in the ocean. Amber is a fossil resin discovered from shore deposits of the Baltic Sea.

Technological advances in industry have resulted in the production of synthetic versions of almost every gemstone. Synthetic gems are identical to natural gems in chemical composition and crystal formation. With some gems, it takes an expert to distinguish between the true stone and the imitation. A deceptive technique sometimes used in the jewelry trade is cementing the top of a hard stone, such as natural quartz or garnet, to a base of glass and using the mount to hide the seam. A gem with a price that seems too good to be true should always be examined before it is set in a mounting.

Whether collected for mystic properties or geologic lessons, rocks, minerals, and gemstones are prized for their natural beauty and the wonder they evoke at our magnificent planet earth.

LEGENDARY AMERICANS

Nancy Skarmeas

John Muir

John Muir, founder of the Sierra Club and leader in establishing our first national parks, changed the way nineteenth-century Americans thought about their environment. He challenged those who would recklessly plunder the nation's abundant natural resources as well as those who pursued conservation in the name of humanity rather than in the name of the environment. Muir was our first true environmental preservationist; he was a man who understood that all life on earth—human, animal, and plant—was interrelated and precious.

Muir was born in Dunbar, Scotland, in 1838. When he was eleven, his family moved to America to farm in Wisconsin. But Muir found his true home in 1868 at age thirty when he first laid eyes on California's Yosemite Valley. Surrounded by the steep, rocky peaks of the Sierra Nevada Mountains, the Yosemite Valley was a harsh and breathtakingly beautiful place which was largely unexplored. Muir approached this territory full of enthusiasm, ready to experience nature on its grandest scale.

A few years earlier, a freak accident at the Indianapolis carriage parts plant where Muir worked had left him temporarily blinded; in his days of darkness Muir vowed that if his sight returned he would devote his entire self to the study and appreciation of the natural world. When he regained his vision, Muir remained true to his promise.

In the Yosemite Valley, Muir found exactly what he was searching for. The natural beauty of the place was unrivaled by anything he had ever encountered, and he quickly became a devoted student of Yosemite. While working for a sheep rancher in the highlands above the valley, he began to understand how unrestricted farming and ranching, which stripped the hillsides of the natural protection of trees and grasses, could damage the environment.

Muir worked as a tour guide in the valley and earned a reputation as a brilliant man with an infinite and intimate knowledge of the region. Among the many scientists, explorers, and tourists who followed his lead through the California mountains was Ralph Waldo Emerson. Emerson and Muir shared the belief that humans were at their best when living close to nature; they became fast friends.

For years Muir kept journals of his travels and experiences. With encouragement from Emerson and others, he began to turn those journals into magazine articles and books. It was his hope to spread his passion for the appreciation and the conservation of nature across America.

While the Yosemite Valley was to remain his true home for the remainder of his days, Muir also expanded his exploration throughout the Northwest and into Alaska, writing more and more as his knowledge and experience increased. No matter where he was, Muir took in the landscape with an open and active mind and the remarkable ability to see the world from a timeless, universal perspective.

In his day many people claimed to be concerned with conservation of natural resources, but their true motive was utilitarian. They argued that the forests and mountains and plains must be protected for human use, to be used, exploited, and consumed. Muir was a new breed of environmentalist. He too was concerned with conservation, but not for the sake of humans alone, but for the sake of all life on earth. Thus Muir saw the need to control the sheep grazing and timber cutting that was devastating the terrain in the Yosemite Valley, despite the claims of the ranchers and loggers that they had a right to their way of life. He understood that without management this very way of life, along with the beautiful environment that supported it, would soon be gone for good. Muir wanted to preserve Yosemite so that future generations could see its spectacular beauty and also because he recognized the interrelatedness of all life on earth. He knew that the loss of any piece of the picture would disrupt the natural order.

John Muir lived in or near the Yosemite Valley for almost a half century. He never tired of its beauty and never felt completely satisfied that enough was being done to preserve it. Through his prolific writings, he shared his appreciation of the beauty of the natural world and his passion for preservation.

Muir's views met with opposition, certainly, but for every voice raised against Muir, several more rallied behind him. Muir's leadership helped secure our first national parks—Yosemite, Sequoia, and General Grant (later renamed Kings Canyon)—and began the movement to preserve land across America. He was also the leader of the small group of environmentalists who founded the Sierra Club in 1892. The club began with the goal of "preserving the forests and other natural features of the Sierra Nevada Mountains" and has since grown into an environmental organization with an international scope and more than 500,000 members. Muir served as the president of the Sierra Club from its founding until his death in 1913.

John Muir, blessed with a second gift of sight, opened the eyes of Americans to a new way of thinking about their land. In the nineteenth century, America seemed limitless and indestructible. Muir had the wisdom and foresight to see that we were on the path to irreversible damage to our landscape. Through his writings and active leadership, he helped to guarantee that the beauty that inspired him throughout his life would stay intact for generations to come. Today, when we see opposition between humanity and the environment, we would do well to look through the eyes of John Muir and see that humanity is inseparable from the environment and what is best for the environment will ultimately be what is best for humanity.

Nature's Creed

Author Unknown

I believe in the brook as it wanders
From hillside into glade;

I believe in the breeze as it whispers
When evening's shadows fade.

I believe in the roar of the river
As it dashes from high cascade;

I believe in the cry of the tempest
'Mid the thunder's cannonade.

I believe in the light of shining stars;
I believe in the sun and the moon;

I believe in the flash of lightning;
I believe in the nightbird's croon;

I believe in the faith of the flowers;
I believe in the rock and sod;

For in all of these appeareth clear
The handiwork of God.

Opposite Page
UPPER YOSEMITE FALLS
Yosemite National Park, California
Jeff Gnass Photography

Overleaf Photograph
YOSEMITE CHAPEL
Yosemite National Park, California
Ron Thomas/FPG International

Lisa C. Thompson

Yosemite National Park
Yosemite, California

The spectacular wilderness that is Yosemite National Park was once a huge expanse of water. As soil slowly eroded from the surrounding mountains, huge rock layers formed and shifted upward to become the Sierra Nevada mountain range. During the Ice Age, grinding glaciers shaped the terrain into the polished domes and deep gorges we see today.

Native Americans first settled in the Yosemite Valley nearly 4,000 years ago. With both Southern Miwok and Mono Lake Paiute ancestry, the native people of Yosemite enjoyed a culture rich in tradition, religion, and song. Their homeland was overtaken in 1849 when gold was discovered in the Sierra Nevada foothills. Today, park visitors can learn more about Yosemite's first settlers at the Indian Village of the Ahwahnee, which is a reconstructed Miwok-Paiute village.

After the gold rush, the influx of humans to the Yosemite Valley alarmed conservationists. They appealed to Congress, and in 1864 President Lincoln signed a bill granting Yosemite Valley and the Mariposa Grove of Giant Sequoias to California as a public trust. The legendary naturalist John Muir soon began campaigning for the protection of the High Sierra meadows as well, which resulted in the federal legislation that created Yosemite National Park in 1890. Muir became known as the "Father of Yosemite" for his lobbying efforts and his writings about this glorious wilderness in eastern California.

Yosemite National Park is part of the legacy of John Muir. His poetic descriptions of its natural beauty come to life when viewing any one of its famous landmarks. A particularly striking example is El Capitan, which is, at 3,593 feet from base to tip, the largest solid granite rock in the world. Yosemite also includes the Mariposa Grove of Giant Sequoias, which are the world's largest living things. With some trees estimated at 3,000 years old, the sequoias are almost the world's oldest, narrowly beaten by the bristlecone pines, which are estimated at 4,000 years old.

In the heart of the park, Yosemite Valley is called "the place of dancing waters" for its nine waterfalls, including Yosemite Falls, the highest waterfall in North America and the second highest in the world. Many of these waterfalls feed into the beautiful Merced River, named "The River of Our Lady of Mercy" by Spanish explorers.

Yosemite also boasts more than seventy-five different species of animals and almost 250 species of birds. Visitors may glimpse a black bear, bobcat, or bighorn sheep roaming in the wild while above soars a red-tailed hawk, great horned owl, or black-backed woodpecker. The animals share the close to 750,000 acres that make up Yosemite, almost ninety-five percent of which is pure wilderness.

Visitors to Yosemite can choose from a diverse range of activities, including a sightseeing tour on an open-air tram, camera walks with a professional photographer, bicycling, guided backpacking, horseback riding, and even rock-climbing. The park touts several galleries, including the Ansel Adams Gallery, and free art classes are available for adults. In the evening you may choose to take a moonlight tour or attend a performance at the Yosemite Theater.

Yosemite National Park is a treasure trove of wilderness wonders preserved more than a century ago for the people of North America. Whether you desire an exhilarating hike to the peak of Cloud's Rest or a tranquil horseback ride through the valley, Yosemite is a magical place to rediscover nature.

CLOUD'S REST PEAK ABOVE THE MERCED RIVER. Yosemite National Park, Yosemite, California. Ed Cooper Enterprises.

Along the river, over the hills, in the ground, in the sky, spring work is going on with joyful enthusiasm, new life, new beauty, unfolding, unrolling in glorious exuberant extravagance, —new birds in their nests, new winged creatures in the air, and new leaves, new flowers, spreading, shining, rejoicing everywhere.

—John Muir
from My First Summer in the Sierra

33

GRETCHEN FARBER ON BALD MOUNTAIN. St. Joe National Forest, Idaho. Photograph courtesy of National Agricultural Library, Forest Service Photographic Collection.

Forest Service Auxiliary Corps

Her house is higher than yours, but her kitchen smaller by far. And her garden! With anxious eyes, all summer she'll watch it, for she knows it is growing ships. It is a war garden surely, thousands of acres in extent, and for the first time last summer she was set to guard it.

It is because there is a war that she's in charge. It hadn't been done before—this sending of women alone to lonely cloud-watching outposts.

The name of Forest Service Auxiliary Corps has not been officially adopted, but its personnel releases men for the armed forces and other work.

Last spring, the Forest Service, realizing that an incessant call for lumber in the war effort was stepping up every possible logging operation in the woods and that there was a corresponding increase in the fire hazard, decided to try women in some of the lookout stations. A few of them went to the Kaniksu National Forest of north Idaho and eastern Washington, a mountainous, heavily timbered region that includes the beautiful primitive reaches above Priest Lake, and others into the St. Joe Forest on the Idaho-Montana divide.

"They did a swell job," hard-bitten rangers admit. "They were conscientious, earnest, in fact so anxious to make good that at first they occasionally reported a fog or early morning mist as smoke."

King's Lake Lookout is in the Kaniksu Forest, and there Mrs. Earl Hupp spent the summer as one of these new forest workers. Lady, her dog, was with her, so also Molly Ann, her little daughter. Their "summer cottage on stilts" was a glass-enclosed room perched on a 50-foot tower above the timber line on King's Mountain.

There are about 177 small panes of glass in the windows of a lookout tower and all must be washed at least once a week. It is essential that they be always spotless; otherwise visibility is reduced.

"That was a drawback," Mrs. Hupp said, "washing those windows and standing on the catwalk outside to do it." (And on one side, where the stairs to the tower come up, that catwalk really is narrow and not railed.)

Water was a problem. "Remember the time you threw away the water—remember," Molly Ann giggled.

"Yes, I remember that night," her mother agreed. "It was late when I heard something or someone prowling about at the base of the tower—I threw a pail of water down—it was only a deer, but it might have been a bear."

Throwing away some of her water supply was a hardship for Mrs. Hupp. You get a healthy respect for water in a lookout post. Springs and streams are

SUPERIOR NATIONAL FOREST, MINNESOTA. Photograph courtesy of National Agricultural Library, Forest Service Photographic Collection.

in the valleys, not on the peaks, and you have to carry water about two miles up the mountain in a canvas backpack which holds five gallons.

"I loved the early morning trips to the spring, with the sun just coming above the horizon," said Gretchen Farber, who is a home economics teacher in a junior high school during the winter months but who served on a lookout in the St. Joe Forest last summer. Miss Farber didn't mind the climb up the tower steps with an armful of wood, either— "Just good exercise," she said.

The girls and women split their own wood. The ranger organization hauls the wood—sawed into stove lengths—to the top of the mountain, but the lookouts had to cut it small enough to use. One of the women didn't like carrying it upstairs with only a hand rail to hang on to, so she rigged up a sling that held a sizable armful and pulled the wood to the top of the tower with a long rope.

Two of the many windows open and are screened to keep hornets, flies, and flying ants from moving in for company. The last can be particularly annoying; they arrive in swarms.

A 60-day or a 75-day ration is supplied to each lookout—also a cookbook—but in the past the men and boys have always had trouble with the cooking end of forestry jobs. This summer—well, just ask a certain fire control supervisor who, on an inspection trip, found a woman lookout waiting for him with a fresh huckleberry pie!

Originally printed in The Christian Science Monitor Magazine, *March 4, 1944.*

Harbingers of Spring

Patricia Clark Willis

As feathered friends were flying
Toward the northern skies,
They sojourned near my window
To rest and socialize.

36

Lansing Christman

Easter turns the renewed life of spring-time into spiritual symbolism of the Resurrection. It is a time of blessed joy and a renewal of our faith in eternal life.

After a winter of rest, it is something to behold when new life comes back to the land. You can witness the rebirth everywhere about you in blossom and birdsong and in new leaf and greening grass.

God's creation is evident in all things, such as the golden sunrise over the eastern hills which marks the coming of a new day just as it has been doing since the beginning of time. I meditate on all that I see and hear, in all that I feel so devoutly within my being.

The gold of spring is a fresh new gold, tender in all its loveliness, different from the autumn gold of goldenrod and falling leaf. The forsythia's yellow blooms form a dome of gold in our yard. A couple of bushes we transplanted at the edge of the woods a few years ago shine as golden as the spring sun. The gold of the dandelions spreads like a ray of sunshine in the green grass. The sunshine brightens the daffodils in the flower bed and highlights the gold of the marsh marigold in the swamp.

The birds sing with joy in celebration of the new life around them—robins and blue-birds, red-winged blackbirds with their scarlet epaulets, mockingbirds, cardinals, and white-throated sparrows. The rose-breasted grosbeak which sports a triangle of rose red on its breast flits through the trees. Accompanying the birdsongs are the tinkling waters of a hillside stream, gently trickling through the seams of the earth. And from the swamps the spring peepers pipe their chords like a chorus of shrill bells announcing the glory of renewed life.

This is a time for the spiritual celebration of the Resurrection. Easter is God's promise of everlasting life to all who put their trust and faith in our Lord and Saviour, Jesus Christ.

The author of two published books, Lansing Christman has been contributing to Ideals *for over twenty years. Mr. Christman has also been published in several American, foreign, and braille anthologies. He lives in rural South Carolina.*

Each Year

May Smith White

Can spring be far away when robins call,
When snowmen gradually withdraw from sight,
When wild geese soar high in northward flight,
Or when autumn's browning leaves
Have ceased to fall?

Today I saw behind the garden wall
Pale greening shoots now coming into light
As if awakened only just last night.
This makes me know that earth
Keeps life in all.

I somehow know when spring is close at hand,
For then I feel within my heart a glow
Of warmth that only special time can bring.
I too see changing colors on the land
Where violets and yellow jasmine grow.
Each year brings forth a bright new
Birth of spring.

TULIP FARM
Mt. Vernon, Washington
Ed Cooper Enterprises

FOR THE CHILDREN
ARTWORK BY RUSS FLINT

WHAT ROBIN TOLD
George Cooper

How do robins build their nests?
Robin Redbreast told me—
First a wisp of yellow hay
In a pretty round they lay,
Then some shreds of downy floss,
Feathers, too, and bits of moss,
Woven with a sweet, sweet song,
This way, that way, and across;
That's what Robin told me.

Where do robins hide their nests?
Robin Redbreast told me—
Up among the leaves so deep,
Where the sunbeams rarely creep,
Long before the winds are cold,
Long before the leaves are gold,
Bright-eyed stars will peep and see
Baby robins—one, two, three;
That's what Robin told me.

The unique perspective of Russ Flint's artistic style has made him a favorite of Ideals *readers for many years. A resident of California and father of four, Russ Flint has illustrated a children's Bible and many other books.*

44

THROUGH MY WINDOW

Pamela Kennedy

A Donkey for a King

"Father, do you think we shall see the temple?" The young boy struggled to keep up with the older man who walked a few paces ahead of him. "Will there be people from all across the world there, Father?"

With an indulgent smile, Simeon stopped walking and turned to face his son. The boy was tugging on the rope tied to the bridle of a most uncooperative young donkey. The animal was determined to stop and nibble on every weed bordering the dusty road to Bethany, and the boy was just as determined to keep moving along.

"Benjamin, your questions will be answered when we arrive in Jerusalem. Be patient, my son. Here, let me help you with Rufus." Simeon yanked a handful of grass from the roadside and waved it under the nose of the reluctant colt. Tantalized by the sweet scent, Rufus snorted once and trotted along after the man.

"I wish Rufus would let us ride him," Benjamin said. "Then we could get there quicker."

Simeon patted the pack on the donkey's back. "I think Rufus has done remarkably well to keep the pack on his back, given his nasty disposition!"

"Oh, he isn't nasty, Father. He just has a mind of his own and doesn't like to be told what to do!"

"Like someone else I know," remarked Simeon, smiling at the flush of red in his son's tanned cheeks.

Benjamin ducked his head and urged Rufus on. "Look Father!" The boy stopped at the top of a small rise and pointed to the small city below. Low stucco residences were bathed in the purple of the twilight. The two travelers picked up their pace and quickly found the home of their relatives, who greeted them with embraces, cool water for their dusty feet, and a hot meal for their empty stomachs. After eating, Benjamin curled up on his sleeping mat and fell asleep, dreaming of the Holy City and the magnificent temple he would see the next day.

Benjamin awoke early and dashed out to check on Rufus. Turning at the sound of his master's footsteps, the donkey nickered in recognition.

"Today we will go into Jerusalem, Rufus," the boy whispered. "I will be able to see the Temple!" Benjamin stroked the donkey's coat, brushing out burrs and bits of grass until the sound of voices nearby interrupted his thoughts.

"Did he say which house?" a man asked.

"No, he just said to go to Bethany and look for a donkey tied at a home near the edge of the city," a second man replied.

"Well, how are we supposed to pay for this mysterious donkey?"

"He just said to take it and, if anyone asks, say 'The Lord needs it.'"

"Look there, by that house on the right. See it?" whispered the first man.

Benjamin stiffened as the men approached.

"Shalom, young man, is this your donkey?" asked one of the men, patting Rufus on the neck.

"Yes, sir," answered Benjamin, wondering if the men were thieves, or worse. His grip tightened on Rufus's bridle, and his heart began to pound. He saw the second man reach for the rope tying Rufus to the olive tree. "Why are you untying my colt?" he demanded.

The first man gently placed his hand on Benjamin's arm and said, "The Lord needs it."

Benjamin couldn't explain the feeling that came over him; but his heart calmed, and his fear dissolved. He untied the rope and then handed it to the man. Rufus gave a quizzical look at his young master but obediently followed the two strangers as they walked down the quiet street.

"You did what?!" Simeon exclaimed when Benjamin related the story to him. "I'll not be getting you another donkey, young man. A fool must learn from his own mistakes. You may now carry our belongings, since you have decided to give Rufus away!" Simeon tossed his pack into Benjamin's arms, shook his head at the boy, and strode off down the road. Benjamin ran to catch up with his father.

Oddly, Benjamin wasn't upset about losing Rufus, but he couldn't explain it to his father because he didn't really understand it himself.

They were joined by other travelers, and soon the road was crowded with excited pilgrims. Benjamin strained to see and hear everything. Ahead of them, there was a commotion. A cloud of golden dust rose from the road, and voices rang out in the hot morning air.

"What is it, Father?" the boy asked excitedly.

"I don't know. Keep close. Don't get lost in the crowd."

They hurried to catch up to the excitement, and Benjamin saw women waving palm branches. Men threw their coats and robes on the roadway, and children shouted, "Blessed is the King who comes in the name of the Lord! Peace in heaven and glory in the highest!"

They were making way for a young man riding on a donkey. Benjamin wriggled through the throng to get a better look. If there were a king going by, Benjamin was not going to miss seeing him! Just as the man came into view Benjamin caught his breath. "Rufus!" he shouted.

The little donkey that had never allowed anyone to sit on his back walked along the Jerusalem road proudly carrying the man called Jesus. As he passed Benjamin, Rufus whinnied softly. Jesus turned and smiled at the boy, then reached down to pat the donkey softly as if to reassure Benjamin that all was well.

Benjamin felt a hand on his shoulder and looked up to see his father. "Look, Father, it's Rufus! Do you know the man who rides him?"

Simeon nodded slowly as he took his son's hand and followed the entourage. "Yes, Benjamin, his name is Jesus, and today we have seen something our ancestors only dreamed of. In the years to come, you will be able to tell your grandchildren that you witnessed something far greater than the Great Temple or the Holy City, for on this day, my son, you saw the Messiah!"

Pamela Kennedy is a free-lance writer of short stories, articles, essays, and children's books. Wife of a naval officer and mother of three children, she has made her home on both U.S. coasts and in Hawaii and currently resides in Washington, D.C. She draws her material from her own experiences and memories, adding bits of her imagination to create a story or mood.

The Triumphant Entry

And it came to pass, when he was
come nigh to Bethphage and
Bethany, at the mount
called the mount
of Olives, he sent two of his disciples, Saying,
Go ye into the village over against you;
in the which at your entering ye shall find a colt tied,
whereon yet never man sat: loose him, and bring him hither.
And if any man ask you, Why do ye loose him?
thus shall ye say unto him,
Because the Lord hath need of him.
And they that were sent went their way,
and found even as he had said unto them.
And as they were loosing the colt,
the owners thereof said unto them,
Why loose ye the colt?
And they said, The Lord hath need of him.
And they brought him to Jesus:
and they cast their garments upon the colt,
and they set Jesus thereon.
And as he went, they spread their clothes in the way.
And when he was come nigh, even now at the descent
of the mount of Olives, the whole multitude of the disciples
began to rejoice and praise God with a loud voice
for all the mighty works that they had seen;
Saying, Blessed be the King that cometh
in the name of the Lord: peace in heaven, and
glory in the highest.

LUKE 19:29-38

Opposite Page
JESUS' TRIUMPHANT ENTRY INTO JERUSALEM
Original painting by Joseph Maniscalco

The Last Supper

Now the first day of the feast
of unleavened bread
the disciples came to Jesus,
saying unto him,
Where wilt thou that we prepare
for thee to eat the passover?
And he said, Go into the city to such a man,
and say unto him,
The Master saith, My time is at hand;
I will keep the passover at thy house with my disciples.
And the disciples did as Jesus had appointed them;
and they made ready the passover.
Now when the even was come, he sat down with the twelve.

And as they were eating, Jesus took bread, and blessed it,
and brake it, and gave it to the disciples, and said,
Take, eat; this is my body.
And he took the cup, and gave thanks,
and gave it to them, saying, Drink ye all of it;
For this is my blood of the new testament,
which is shed for many for the remission of sins.
But I say unto you, I will not drink henceforth of this fruit
of the vine, until that day when I drink it new with you
in my Father's kingdom.

MATTHEW 26:17-20; 26-29

The Garden

And he came out, and went,
as he was wont,
to the mount of Olives;
and his disciples
also followed him. And when he was at the place,
he said unto them,
Pray that ye enter not into temptation.
And he was withdrawn from them about a stone's cast,
and kneeled down, and prayed,
Saying, Father, if thou be willing,
remove this cup from me: nevertheless not my will,
but thine, be done.
And there appeared an angel unto him from heaven,
strengthening him.
And being in an agony he prayed more earnestly:
and his sweat was as it were great drops of blood
falling down to the ground.
And when he rose up from prayer,
and was come to his disciples,
he found them sleeping for sorrow.

LUKE 22:39-45

Opposite Page
THE AGONY IN THE GARDEN
Original painting by Joseph Maniscalco

The Betrayal

And while he yet spake, lo, Judas,
one of the twelve,
came, and with him
a great multitude
with swords and staves, from the chief priests
and elders of the people.
Now he that betrayed him gave them a sign, saying,
Whomsoever I shall kiss, that same is he: hold him fast.
And forthwith he came to Jesus,
and said, Hail, master; and kissed him.
And Jesus said unto him,
Friend, wherefore art thou come?
Then came they, and laid hands on Jesus, and took him.
And, behold, one of them which were with Jesus
stretched out his hand, and drew his sword,
and struck a servant of the high priest's,
and smote off his ear.
Then said Jesus unto him,
Put up again thy sword into his place:
for all they that take the sword
shall perish with the sword.

MATTHEW 26:47-52

The Trial

Then Pilate entered
into the judgment
hall again, and called Jesus,
and said unto him,
Art thou the King of the Jews?
Jesus answered him, Sayest thou this thing of thyself,
or did others tell it thee of me?
Pilate answered, Am I a Jew?
Thine own nation and the chief priests
have delivered thee unto me: what hast thou done?
Jesus answered, My kingdom is not of this world:
if my kingdom were of this world,
then would my servants fight,
that I should not be delivered to the Jews:
but now is my kingdom not from hence.
Pilate therefore said unto him,
Art thou a king then?
Jesus answered, Thou sayest that I am a king.
To this end was I born,
and for this cause came I into the world,
that I should bear witness unto the truth.
Every one that is of the truth heareth my voice.

JOHN 18:33-37

Opposite Page
CHRIST BEFORE PILATE
Original painting by Joseph Maniscalco

The Crucifixion

And Pilate answered and said
again unto them,
What will ye then that
I shall do unto him
whom ye call the King of the Jews?
And they cried out again,
Crucify him.
Then Pilate said unto them,
Why, what evil hath he done?
And they cried out the more exceedingly,
Crucify him.
And so Pilate, willing to content the people,
released Barabbas unto them,
and delivered Jesus, when he had scourged him,
to be crucified.

And they clothed him with purple,
and platted a crown of thorns, and put it about his head,
And began to salute him, Hail, King of the Jews!
And they smote him on the head with a reed,
and did spit upon him,
and bowing their knees worshipped him.
And when they had mocked him,
they took off the purple from him,
and put his own clothes on him,
and led him out to crucify him.
And it was the third hour,
and they crucified him.

MARK 15:12-15; 17-20; 25

The Resurrection

But Mary stood without at
the sepulchre weeping:
and as she wept,
she stooped down,
and looked into the sepulchre,
And seeth two angels in white sitting,
the one at the head, and the other at the feet,
where the body of Jesus had lain.
And they say unto her, Woman, why weepest thou?
She saith unto them, Because they have taken away my Lord,
and I know not where they have laid him.
And when she had thus said, she turned herself back,
and saw Jesus standing, and knew not that it was Jesus.
Jesus saith unto her, Woman, why weepest thou?
whom seekest thou? She, supposing him to be the gardener,
saith unto him, Sir, if thou have borne him hence,
tell me where thou hast laid him, and I will take him away.
Jesus saith unto her, Mary.
She turned herself, and saith unto him,
Rabboni; which is to say, Master.
Jesus saith unto her, Touch me not;
for I am not yet ascended to my Father:
but go to my brethren, and say unto them,
I ascend unto my Father, and your Father;
and to my God, and your God.

JOHN 20:11-17

Opposite Page
THE TWO MARYS AT THE EMPTY TOMB
Original painting by Joseph Maniscalco

Golden Bells

E. June Mathews

The daffodils awoke with joy
And flashed their ruffled gowns of gold;
Though feet were held in captive clay,
They proudly smiled in freezing cold.

The graceful, regal queens are born
As noble blooms of early spring.
The fragile beauties bravely wave
Though Jack invades with frosty sting.

They sing their song on Easter morn
And their day
As b ells
I

BITS & PIECES

"Christ the Lord is risen today,"
Sons of men and angels say.
Raise your joys and triumphs high;
Sing, ye heavens, and earth, reply.
Charles Wesley

And Jesus said unto them, I am the bread of life:
he that cometh to me shall never hunger;
and he that believeth on me shall never thirst.
John 6:35

To see a world in a grain of sand
    And a Heaven in a wild flower,
Hold Infinity in the palm of your hand
    And Eternity in an hour.
William Blake

Nature is too thin a screen;
the glory of the omnipresent God
bursts through everywhere.
Ralph Waldo Emerson

Prayer is the beginning and the middle
and the end of all good: prayer illumineth the soul,
and thereby doth the soul distinguish good from evil.
St. Francis

The more we live by our intellect,
the less we understand the meaning of life.
William James

Let me tonight look back across the span
'Twixt dawn and dark, and to my conscience say—
Because of some good act to beast or human—
"The world is better that I lived today."
Ella Wheeler Wilcox

Dear Lord, I do not ask that life
May always easy be,
But that I always may have strength
For all that comes to me.
Mae E. Margrat

65

Ideals' Family Recipes

Favorite Recipes from the Ideals Family of Readers

Editor's Note: If you would like us to consider your favorite recipe, please send a typed copy of the recipe along with your name and address to *Ideals* Magazine, ATTN: Recipes, P.O. Box 148000, Nashville, Tennessee 37214-8000. We will pay $10 for each recipe used. Recipes cannot be returned.

HOLIDAY BROWN BREAD

In a large mixing bowl, combine 1½ cups raisins, 1 cup granulated sugar, and 1 tablespoon butter or margarine. Pour 1½ cups boiling water over mixture. Cover and set aside for 8 to 10 hours or overnight.

In a large mixing bowl, combine 2¼ cups flour, 2 teaspoons baking soda, and ½ teaspoon light salt. Add to raisin mixture along with 1 egg, beaten, and 1 cup walnut pieces. Mix well by hand.

Remove the labels from three 11-ounce nut cans; coat the insides with non-stick cooking spray and line completely with wax paper, being careful not to rip it. Pour batter into prepared cans to about ⅔ full. Cover with aluminum foil. Bake in a preheated 350° oven for 50 to 60 minutes or until toothpick inserted into center of loaves comes out clean.

Cool in cans on wire rack 15 minutes. (Note: to remove the loaves, open the bottoms of the cans with a can-opener and slide the bread out.) Leave in wax paper until ready to serve to preserve moisture.

Martha Jean Van Dam
Greenwood, Indiana

MY FAVORITE BANANA BREAD

In a large mixing bowl, cream 1 cup granulated sugar with ½ cup butter or margarine. Add two eggs, beaten, and 1 cup mashed banana; mix well. Set aside.

In a large mixing bowl, sift together 2 cups flour, ½ teaspoon salt, and 1 teaspoon baking soda. Add to creamed mixture alternately with ½ cup buttermilk, mixing well after each addition. Fold in ½ cup chopped walnuts.

Pour into greased 8 x 4 x 3-inch bread pan and bake in a preheated 350° oven for 1 hour or until toothpick inserted into center of bread comes out clean.

Cool loaf completely in pan on wire rack. Wrap loaf in foil and store in refrigerator.

Judy Tutor
Molina, Colorado

COTTAGE CHEESE "BUTTERHORNS"

In a large mixing bowl, combine 1 cup butter or margarine and 1 pound small curd creamy cottage cheese, both at room temperature. Cream until light and fluffy. Gradually stir in 2 cups flour and ½ teaspoon salt. Beat with mixer until smooth. Cover and chill overnight.

Divide dough into 4 parts. Roll each part of dough into a circle about ⅛ inch thick. Cut each circle into 12 wedges. Starting at the widest end, roll each wedge toward the point.

Place "butterhorns" point side down on ungreased cookie sheet. Bake in preheated 350° oven 20 to 30 minutes. Cool and frost with thin powdered sugar icing.

Helen Thayer
Madison, Wisconsin

POWDERED SUGAR ICING

In a mixing bowl, combine 2 cups powdered sugar, sifted, and 2 tablespoons butter or margarine, softened; mix thoroughly with a spoon. Stir in ¼ teaspoon vanilla and 2 tablespoons milk. Stir in additional milk, 1 teaspoon at a time, until icing is smooth and of drizzling consistency.

Sparrow's Sweet Song of Spring

Nancy Merical

O tiny sparrow on your perch,
  A silhouette against a darkened sky,
Your lilting song stirs deep a hope in me
  That winter's past and welcome spring is nigh.

Who would think that from your throat,
    So miniature and feathered brown and plain,
Would come a song as sweet as angels' harps,
    E'en though you sing midst cold, damp winter's rain?

Strong March winds will soon transform
    To breezes soft and gentle on my brow,
And I will swiftly run through sylvan glade,
    Ecstatic at the sight of newborn flower.

But for now I respite find
    In trilling song of joy at winter's end
And join your melody of pure delight
    At spring's approach, wee silver-throated friend.

Frontiers of Faith

Mary Linton

Deep in the frozen earth, beneath the crust
Of ice, beneath the cold, unyielding snow,
April waits eagerly, alert. She must
Reach up, and yet how can young April know
There will be sunshine and warm rain to meet
Her struggling efforts toward the light? What real
Assurance does she have against defeat?
The hardened clod, the unrelenting seal
That frost has placed across the waiting land,
Gives little promise of a singing day
When she shall push firm earth aside to stand
Facing with confidence the open way.
But having watched the wealth all Aprils find,
Vast new frontiers of faith possess the mind.

SPRING IN NEW HAMPSHIRE

Claude McKay

Too green the springing April grass,
    Too blue the silver-speckled sky,
For me to linger here, alas,
    While happy winds go laughing by,
Wasting the golden hours indoors,
    Washing windows and scrubbing floors.

Too wonderful the April night,
    Too faintly sweet the first May flowers,
The stars too gloriously bright,
    For me to spend the evening hours,
When fields are fresh and streams are leaping,
    Wearied, exhausted, dully sleeping.

PINK AND WHITE AZALEA BLOSSOMS. Orton, North Carolina. Johnson's Photography.

Azaleas

If I had to prepare a list of "Great Gardening Thrills," I know what I'd put at the very top: the first breathtaking glimpse each spring of a brilliant blooming bank of azaleas.

Even though my childhood was spent in the South, I don't recall ever being impressed with azaleas until I was in high school and living in Japan. Early one spring, my Dad took our family to a mountain resort where I was astonished to see what looked like red-orange neon lights glowing on the mountainsides. The "lights" turned out to be wild azaleas in a stunning profusion of color. Not until I saw wild rhododendrons blooming in the Smoky Mountains did I have a similar experience.

Azaleas and rhododendrons are of the same family—a fact that can be confusing because all azaleas

are rhododendrons but not all rhododendrons are azaleas. Many azaleas are native to the southern highlands; but most of the azaleas that are sold in garden centers today are hybrids of hardy Japanese and Korean species, many of which are evergreens. Some of the most popular of these are the Kurume azaleas, which are hardy to -5° to -10°, although evergreen species are not usually as winter hardy as the deciduous species. Some hybrids, such as the Kaempferi, are evergreen in warm climates but become deciduous by habit in colder weather.

Luckily for northern gardeners, hybridizers are continually developing varieties that are more cold tolerant than their ancestors. One such breeding program resulted in the Glenn Dale hybrids, some 450 cultivars hardy to -10°. Another line of hybrids was developed in New Jersey by crossing cold-tolerant Kurume and Kaempferi hybrids with others to produce the Linwood hybrids, hardy down to -15°.

Azaleas can thrive from Florida all the way up to coastal New England and across the Midwest in a line that includes Lower Michigan, parts of Wisconsin, the southern portions of Iowa and Nebraska, and eastern Colorado. Thanks to the warming effect of the Pacific Ocean, azaleas are hardy up the West Coast as far as Washington and inland to the lower elevations of western Montana.

And what if you don't live in one of these areas? Azaleas thrive in greenhouses, and if you have a garage, you can plant them in containers and simply put them out of sight for the winter. Container growing also provides some interesting pruning possibilities; azaleas make great bonsai trees.

The greatest cause of failure of newly planted azaleas is hot sun. Beginning gardeners often pick the sunniest site they can find, lovingly set out their new plants, and then watch them burn up in July. Azalea culture is easy if you think about how the plants grow in the wild. They almost always grow on sloping ground under the shelter of tall, deciduous trees. Thus they have the benefit of sun in spring, when it is still far to the south. Yet in summer, when the sun is directly overhead, a canopy of trees can protect the azalea from the sun's hotter, more damaging rays.

It's also important to provide protection from prevailing winds in winter. For this reason, azaleas generally do better when planted on the east side of a dwelling or garden wall where they are shaded not only from late afternoon sun but also from howling winter winds.

Drying winds, both winter and summer, can damage the wintergreen varieties of azaleas severely. An easy way to protect them is to spray them at the beginning of the season with an anti-desiccant spray. The spray coats the leaves with a waxy substance that helps prevent transpiration, which is the evaporation of plant moisture into the atmosphere.

The azalea demands an acid soil. This is another reason it does well under tall, deciduous trees. Decaying fallen leaves around established shade trees produce a more acidic soil, so the addition of compost and peat moss is recommended.

Azaleas also require good drainage. Since the soil under tall trees is often compacted, azaleas do best in the wild when they grow on sloping sides of hills and ravines. You can duplicate these conditions by planting your plants on raised mounds, which also gives you more control over soil type.

Another enemy of azaleas are spider mites. Once the plant is attacked, its leaves will start to look pale and mottled. If you run your finger along the underside of a leaf and feel a gritty, dust-like texture, spider mites are at work. A strong stream from a garden hose will knock down most of these pests, and an organically safe spray of insecticidal soap will prevent further problems.

Most azalea varieties are slow growers and light feeders. A top dressing each spring with several inches of compost will provide all the necessary nutrients, or if you choose a commercial fertilizer, look for one specially formulated for azaleas and rhododendrons. Apply fertilizer only in early spring, from February to about mid-April.

If you have fed your plant regularly and its leaves begin to turn yellow, it is probably suffering from chlorosis. The nitrogen in the soil is not in a form the plant can absorb, and thus it loses its color. The condition can be remedied by spraying the plant with a solution of chelated iron. The substance in powder form can also be applied around the drip line of the plant. But handle it carefully: the residue will permanently stain any clothing it touches. I know this for a fact, and I can show you the evidence!

The importance of watering your azalea adequately cannot be over emphasized because the azalea has a very shallow root system. The roots lie so close to the surface that dry summer weather can quickly wipe them out.

Since cultivation can so easily damage the plant's roots, mulching is important. A thick layer of mulch will prevent weeds as well as conserve soil moisture. But be careful not to bury the roots too deeply under the mulch. A mistake many gardeners make is just to pile on additional mulch each year when the previous layer becomes unattractive. Instead, gently rake the old mulch away and add a fresh layer each spring. It's the least you can do for such a remarkable beauty.

Deana Deck lives in Nashville, Tennessee, where her garden column is a regular feature in The Tennessean.

Little Dandelion

Loise Pinkerton Fritz

'Tis March, and, little dandelion,
　　You pop up nice and green;
You'll make a very tasty dish
　　When you are washed and cleaned.

With pail and knife, folks soon will scan
　　The fields and hillsides fair;
You're a perfect springtime tonic,
　　All country folk declare.

Soon March will scamper on its way,
　　Then April will bring showers,
And if May finds you standing still,
　　You'll sport bright yellow flowers.

Your brilliant carpet beautifies
　　The earth when winter's gone.
But please stay on the fields and hills
　　And bypass our front lawn!

Opposite Page
FARMYARD BLOSSOMS
Coon Valley, Wisconsin
Ken Dequaine Photography